Dream BIG Never Small

The Story of Terise Ashley Smith

TERISE ASHLEY SMITH

Dedication Page

To Grandma Floree,

You'll always be my grandma, even in heaven.

Love you,

Your granddaughter, Terise

Hope you're proud of me.

God is within her
she will not fail
Psalm 46:5

To: The Conscious Route

I hope you are encouraged
to Go HARD for your dreams!

love,

Terise Ashley Smith

Table Of Contents

Foreword xi

Chapter 1 – #TeriseTheDancer 1

Chapter 2 – #TeriseTheModel 7

Chapter 3 – #TeriseTheActress 15

Chapter 4 – #TeriseTheGiver 21

Chapter 5 – #TeriseTheOvercomer 23

Chapter 6 – Mommy's Chapter – #TheProudMom 29

Chapter 7 – #InspirationReallyIsEverywhere 33

Chapter 8 – #TeriseTheArtistAndOrangeBelt 39

Chapter 9 – Learning to Ride My Bike 43

Chapter 10 – #MyFinalMessage 47

Hello everybody!!

My name is Terise Ashley Smith. I'm 8 years old, in the third grade, at a Baltimore County Public School. The purpose of this book is to share with you the gifts that I've been blessed with by God.

The things that I am working on today will help me prepare for my BIG DREAM …. Being on Broadway! Walking the Runway in places like Paris and NYC, being on TV or even

BIGGER…. Movies!!! Yes, I believe that **I CAN DO** all of this and so can you…… So read my journey and hopefully I can encourage **EVERYONE to DREAM BIG and NEVER SMALL** !!!

Acknowledgments

I want to say THANK YOU to my Pastor, Apostle Dr. Karen S. Bethea, my dance teachers, Ms. Madison, Mrs. Staci & Ms. Kiana, dance studio owner, Ms. A, my model coach Ms. Thee Danielle Baker, my acting coach Mr. Brian, my Taekwondo instructor Mr. Tony, my book mentor Ms. Kimmoly who helped me from start to finish with this book, and Ms. Mary, my website creator & the President of #TeamTerise LOL, for all your support!!!

Of course I want to THANK my mommy & daddy!

Looooooove ya'll, my family in NYC, NC and FL, everyone in BALTIMORE (Go Ravens!!), my church family, Set the Captives Free Outreach Center, my Principals, teachers and friends at school, all my friends at Studio "A" and the many people who follow me on Facebook, Twitter, Instagram and YouTube under @ ThisIsTerise #LoveYall!!

Thank you Gabrielle Jordan for the inspiration!!!

TOGETHER …. **WE ARE** #TeamTerise

Foreword

From the moment I met Terise Ashley Smith, I knew that she was special. Not just because she's gifted, talented and very intelligent. As if that's not enough. But from the onset of our student / pupil relationship, I noticed that she had an incredible heart. Her passion for God, her family and others exudes from her in a very unique way.

If you've ever spent an extended period of time around young people, they typically have several things on their mind, themselves and having fun. And while Terise is a normal, fun loving child, she also displays a unique magnetic quality that draws her to others in need and others to her as well. On far too many occasions to count, I have witnessed her thinking about, caring for, and sacrificing her time and resources for others. Many times we categorize leaders as those who have the innate ability to inspire and guide others. And while Terise possess those qualities as well, the real essence of a leader is that they have a heart to serve others. That's Terise Ashley Smith.

Another important aspect of leadership is not fearing huge moments or great tasks that stand in front of you. There is a wonderful children's song that says "I might as well THINK BIG. Why should any thought be small? I might as well

THINK BIG if I'm going to think at all". In a day and time when our children are exposed to so many negative images and messages via TV, radio and social media which strongly contribute to them being uninspired, stagnant and misguided, it is so refreshing to hear such inspiring and motivating words from an impressive future leader.

In this amazing first- hand account of her young life, Terise Ashley Smith reminds her readers both young and old that it is absolutely never too soon or too late to become a dreamer. Through her honest and revealing God inspired testimony, Terise shares how she courageously faces and overcomes life's daily challenges. In similar fashion, not only does she fearlessly proclaim her lofty goals and aspirations, but also boldly describes how she plans to transform her impressive dreams into reality. In its simplest form, Terise manages to take the meaningful words of the above mentioned song and somehow through her young prophetic voice, take them to an even more profound level. I am confident that after you and your child read this book, you will not only be motivated and inspired to elevate your thinking, but to also Dream BIG Never Small.

Antonio M. Watson, Sr.
Owner
& Chief Instructor
Powerhouse Taekwondo

Chapter 1

#TeriseTheDancer

*I*started dancing when I was 5 years old. I wanted to take classes earlier, but mommy was like "If I'm paying for it, you need to be able to show me what you've learned and not just twirling on the stage". She was serious too!

Mommy knew of a young African American Ballerina named Michaela DePrince. She thought Michaela would be a good dance role model for me. She was someone that would get me pumped up and excited about dance and not wanna quit after a month of classes. I started looking at all her videos on Youtube and she was right! I was soooooo inspired by Michaela, (a former dancer with the Dance Theatre of Harlem). Watching her dance on pointe shoes got me EXCITED!!! One of my favorite and I mean favorite videos of her was this dance that she did with a tambourine. She would hit that tambourine, on Pointe shoes, like 5 times, back to back. I've never seen a dancer do that before!!! After seeing her dance on pointe, I KNEW that one day, if I continued to practice hard, I would also be able to dance on pointe shoes….. one day.

Lesson from Mommy

If you look for it, you will find that Inspiration is everywhere... even on YouTube!!

In 2012 I began to take Ballet, Modern and most recently, Tap classes and Hip Hop at Studio "A" Modeling, Etiquette and Dance Academy.

Since I've been a Studio "A" dancer I've learned a lot of new dance vocabulary words, some real easy moves and some really hard moves, like Pirouettes, Passe', Battement (bat-MAHN) , Tendu and heel stretches. My teachers and Ms. A, the owner, have a lot of patience with me and want to see me reach my goals. I even was given a certificate for being a leader, showing progress and hard work. How cool was that!! #MyFirstRecital with my dance studio, was December of 2012. I performed in our version of the "Nutcracker". I was afraid I would mess up, but thank God I didn't. After the show, my mom was waiting for me with balloons and flowers. It was the best moment ever....my first recital DONE!! I danced my FIRST solo at a Fashion Show for my model coach, Ms. Danielle. Of course now, when I dance, I never want the recital to

#MyFirstSolo #VideoOnMyYoutubePage

end! #LifeOfADancer. Today, I perform in recitals every December, June and August.

Ok.... so that was the good and now I have to tell you some of the not so good.

One day, I came to class and I was really upset because I realized my friends moved up a level and I was like "ummmm, where ya'll going"?? They said "class"!!! I ran to my mom and was like, "Mommy, why are my friends in class right now without me"? She said "Terise, I don't know". With a really sad face, I said "I think they moved up a level". I begged my mom to talk to my teacher to find out why I didn't move up, but she said, "Terise, if you want to know, YOU or me AND you can talk to Ms. Madison together". I was really nervous because I wasn't sure what she was going to say.

After listening to what Ms. Madison said I felt discouraged.... just a little bit... but I realized I had to work harder and not focus on what my friends were doing. My mom talked to me later and showed me a quote from Maya

Angelou. The quote said "all great achievements require time". This means to me all the things you want, you can't rush. Practice, Practice and more Practice will definitely get you to where you want to be. I have to be honest, this is a hard lesson for an 8 year old, but I think I understand now.

Meeting Michaela DePrince – My Dance Inspiration

We first met on Twitter, believe it or not, LOL. I know ya'll are probably like, "Terise, you have a Twitter account"?? YUP, and Facebook, Youtube, Instagram AND a website!! #SocialMediaOnFleek. The hashtag on Twitter one day was #PeopleIdLikeToMeet. I tweeted her, @MichDePrince with the hashtag and screamed SO loud when she tweeted me back!!! After several tweets, my mom and Michaela arranged for me to have a PRIVATE LESSON at the Dance Theatre of Harlem in NYC!!! OMG, I couldn't believe I was going to meet her!! That day, and that session, was AMAZING! She gave me good tips and told me to continue to point and flex my toes everyday (it's helpful for all ballet dancers). We continued to stay in touch over Twitter and one day my mom said she was coming to Baltimore to perform and of course, we bought tickets. When I first saw Michaela dance in person, I was speechless!! She was the prettiest dancer ever!!! Seeing her after the show made me happy to know that she remembered

me. I got in the car and cried!! I was HAPPY!!!

Lesson from Terise

Who do you look up too that is doing something you want to do??

Find someone and #GetInspired!!

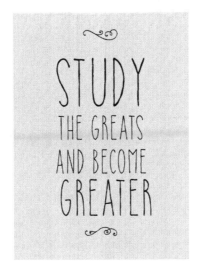

Chapter 2

~

#TeriseTheModel

So, I started modeling when I was 3 years old. My modeling coach is Ms Thee Danielle Baker. She helps me with my modeling, posing, facial expressions, how to speak in front of a camera, how to give a good interview and so much more. She's even writing her own book called "Model Behavior". #StayTuned

Some of the fashion shows I've been in were Baltimore Fashion Week, Lord and Taylor Back to School show, Maryland Fashion Week and I can't forget fashion shows for Ms. Danielle's 2 businesses, Girls GLAM and Signature Ink. Modeling is my passion BECAUSE I can wear make-up, try on all these really cute clothes and I can be myself and be a girly girl!!! I love being who I am... I love myself ....I'm worth a lot.

I'm not nervous being in front of the camera or on the runway because I'm used to being in front of a whole LOT OF PEOPLE . As long as you're confident and have your head held high, you can do it!! One of my favorite fashion shows was Maryland Fashion Week because I got to do a show in Six Flags Great Adventure, which was FUN!!! Afterwards, of course, mommy let me ride some of the rides. Can't be all work and not have fun, right? LOL. I walked for three designers that day. One was a jewelry designer who put really cute jewelry on my skin.

I don't like to watch fashions shows; I like to be IN the fashion shows. One time I went to watch a Girls Glam fashion show. All my friends were in the show. We call them Glammies. I felt sad that I wasn't in the show, but supportive of all my glammies.

My favorite photo shoot was an outdoor shoot that I did with Ms. Danielle. I wore a green tutu (I love tutus ☺). I was in the middle of Baltimore City on Charles Street. I remember saying to my mom and Ms. Danielle that I wanted everyone to stop and watch…. Oh and clap and be like "nice job Terise". What can I say……. I love to perform in front of an audience.

Photographer – Thee Danielle Baker

I also did a photo shoot with Jazzy Studios, Mr. Jeff and Ms. Aisha, LOVE THEM!! Ms. Aisha asked me if I could do a pose on my toes, kinda like what Michael Jackson would do. I said "Yeah, I can do that…I think". She started to count down 3..2…1…GO!! Then again… 3…2…1….GO!! I wasn't really sure what the picture was going to look like but I did it anyway. Ms. Aisha showed me the pic on her camera and I was like WOW!!! I can't believe I did a pose like that. I was SPEECHLESS!! I LOVED IT! I felt like I could do anything I put my mind to. It was my first time doing a pose like that. I was PROUD of myself.

Lesson from Terise

Don't be afraid to try new things ... even if you don't know if you can do it or not .... JUST TRY!!

Photographer – Aisha Butler / Jazzy Studios

#BamWhat!!! I got that from Liv and Maddie, a TV show on the Disney Channel.

My biggest accomplishments as a model were being on the August 2012 cover of Baltimore's

Child!! The magazine was everywhere....My church, my preschool, supermarkets and even the library!!! Can you imagine being 5 years old and seeing yourself every time you went to the market and the library for a whole 30 days!! Well, it happened to me and it was THE BEST FEELING EVER!! I was also blessed to be in the winter edition of Tween Girl Style Magazine. They sent my mom the questions they wanted me to answer. I had a photoshoot with Ms. Danielle, sent the pictures and the answers back to Tween Girl and there it was .... My FIRST

ARTICLE!! #GodIsAmazing. I also had an opportunity to do a photo shoot for the Maryland Science Center. The pictures were used in their 2014 Summer Camp pamphlet. My mom called the marketing director and was able to get 4 copies for us and the family!!

<u>Update from Terise</u>** – My mother showed me a video one day on the computer. It was a commercial for the Maryland Science Center. I was in the video!!!! .....but then she also told me the commercial was on TV!!! I haven't seen the commercial on TV yet, but if I did….. I would feel REALLY PROUD of myself and I'd probably cry!!! ** #YessssReese #DreamsCanComeTrue

In 2014, I had the opportunity to compete, for the first time, in modeling at the World Championships of Performing Arts in California. I had one roommate and her name was Briana and her mom, Ms. Monica. We stayed there for 11 days at the Westin Hotel. I also got to see the Hollywood sign! I won three medals, they were gold, bronze and silver. I was so proud of myself but I told myself not to show off because some people didn't win anything.

My mom told me one day that Ms. Danielle wanted me to be a guest on her radio show for "Model Appreciation Month". I was so excited to be on the radio with my friend Aria from Girls GLAM. My 1st radio interview!! We had equipment like headphones, microphones and a video camera. I really loved talking about myself and all the things I had done. I was so excited, I didn't want to leave … at all!!

We had people call in and ask us questions. My mom even answered questions about being a "Model Mom".

The interview was on the same day as my MRI (see chapter 5 #TeriseTheOvercomer). It was a rough start, but my day ended AMAZING. The lesson is to overcome your fears and to be BRAVE! I woke up having a bad day and didn't want to go to my doctor's appointment. I was sad for a short time, but in the end, I had a great day!!

I always go to school; mommy always says #SchoolComesFirst. One day she told me that I had to miss school for a casting call in Philadelphia. I've never been to

Philadelphia before. We drove kinda far, but the judges were really nice AND they were really impressed with my model walk. Once it was over, I had to wait until they emailed me to say yes or no. My mom told me a long time ago that whenever I try out for anything, there are only 2 answers, YES or NO. "You either get it or you don't". I definitely understand that now.

Monday when I woke up, mommy told me the good news; I got in the fashion show!!! #OhYeah , my FIRST show outside of Maryland!! I used to travel to NY for casting calls and never got anything. When I don't get stuff, I'm sad....but I say "I didn't get it, but I tried". But this time, I GOT IN!!!

Lesson from Terise

You might be sad that sometimes you don't get stuff you want, but I KNOW that if you keep going and follow your dreams, one day you can get an email that says

"CONGRATULATIONS",
just like I did !!!

UPDATE from mommy** Schedule conflicts happen ALL THE TIME in the Arts Industry. So unfortunately, the day of the mandatory rehearsal for the fashion show, where the designers were to pick their models, Terise was at The Murphy Fine Arts Center performing in her Spring Recital. We are still very proud of Terise for being selected. We also wished her friends from Girls Glam that were also in the show, much success.**

Chapter 3

~

#TeriseTheActress

My acting coach is Mr. Brian. He is also a member of my church, Set the Captives Free Outreach Center.

Mr. Brian is so talented. My mom says he's like Baltimore's own Tyler Perry, LOL. He plays the organ, piano, sings, writes plays and music, and he teaches.

He started an acting class for young people like me called Xpressions Academy. My friends in Xpressions were Bethanny, Ethan, Meagan, Morgan and Nia. We learned acting tools like warm up drills, impromptu drills, how to project and of course how to BE the character.

At the end of our Xpressions semester, we put on a showcase for our parents. We performed this really cute skit called "I can do anything better than you". It was girls vs. boys . The boys were, of course, saying they could be better than us girls (yeah, right! LOL!

#GirlsRULE). We sang the song AND acted it out at the same time. Not easy doing both… but we did GREAT!! That was my first time performing a creative movement piece.

I have a lot of great acting memories. Once in NYC, I taped a show called YogaPalooza. It was a really fun "circus episode" where we learned different yoga positions & yoga phrases. The show is currently being aired on the Z Living Network. I have my fingers crossed that my episode will air!

My church put on a play called "Carol of the Belles" (written by my acting coach, Mr. Brian) where I played Tori, the daughter of the main character Carol. My friend Bethany played my fake cousin. The play was about my fake mother being on drugs but her mom is trying to stop the habit. She ends up in the hospital because of the drugs but they blamed it on her two friends Tracey and Michael. It was my first time being in a play where I had LOTS of lines, I had to wear a microphone and the costume changes were CRAZY!! We had to change so fast that my real mom had to help me backstage and guess what? I even had to SING. I sang a song called "How it used to be". I tried not to smile when I looked in Tara's eyes (my fake cousin) because it was a sad song. We performed the play on New Year's Eve 2014 and again 2 days later. It was LIGHTS… CAMERA … ACTION at STCF. I loooved being on stage performing. My Aunty Alison and my cousin Aubrey came, Ms. Ro, Ms. Monica and my friends from Studio "A" all came to see me perform. A few weeks later, we had a watch party at Mr. Brian's house where the cast all got together to eat, laugh and watch ourselves on TV. I'd never seen myself on TV before so watching the play on the flat screen was cool, especially after rehearsing the play for so many weeks.

I used to go to New York City for auditions a lot when I had a manager. I felt excited because you can get more acting jobs in NY, BUT, I felt sad because if I didn't get a part, I felt like I wasted all my time traveling. Waiting for the bus was long because you had to stand outside in the rain or snow or a chilly day and the line was TOO much. When we got to NY, it was always CROWDED because all those people had to go somewhere. I HATED it when somebody would push me. It was like everyone was a BUSY BEE, especially on the train and on the streets!!!! I'd be like, "EXCUSE ME…WHERE ARE ALL THESE PEOPLE GOING"?

Going to auditions is really nerve wrecking because I never know what the casting directors are looking for. I don't know if somebody in the room is better than me but I

ALWAYS HAVE HELD MY HEAD HIGH AND TRIED MY BEST!! As of right now, I haven't booked any jobs in NY, but my GOAL is to get a NY agent that will help me find auditions and HOPEFULLY get me on TV shows OR maybe, some movies!!

When you get a lead role, it's a lot because you have to remember a lot of lines, but the GOOD thing is, nobody knows when you forget a line! You can make something up to remember (that's called ad lib). One day my mom was on Instagram and she saw that they were looking for kid actors to film Stiletto Dreams. So my mom said, "I think we should go to the audition". Good, because I was picked to be Young Sam and this other girl played Young Brooke.

Stiletto Dreams is about a girl named Samantha and her best friend Brooke. They are walking home from school and Sam sees boxes to move to New York. Sam felt sad to leave her friend Brooke. I understand because I felt sad when I had to leave my best friend. Her name is Trinity and she moved to New Jersey ®. I've know her since kindergarten. We always wanted to hang out together.

When I saw pics from the movie of me and Young Brooke, I felt sad because it really made me miss Trinity ® Filming Stiletto Dreams outside in the cold was tiring. We had to say the same lines over and over again......AND it started raining. Can ya'll believe that? I know I couldn't. It was my first film and even in the rain, I had fun!!

__Update from mommy__ ... **On October 10th 2015 the Film made its PUBLIC DEBUT in front of a New York City audience. For all updates on the film, follow Stiletto Dreams on Instagram under @Stiletto.Dreams.**

So that was the good! Let me tell you this one thing, that was kind of an OMG moment. I was watching Project Runway one night, then all of a sudden this Macy's Sunday Sale commercial came on. I saw my friend!! I could not believe my eyes. I met her at the Fashion Awards of Maryland 2014. We were both nominated for the "Rising Star" award and she won! ☹ ☹ I had my mom pause the TV then rewind it. I ran around the room SCREAMING AND FREAKING OUT!!! I was jealous, mad, upset and crying.

"Because it's not fair she's only 5, I'm 8, she's on TV and I'm not? Urrggghhh!!!" I called my modeling coach, Ms. Danielle, she said, "When GOD says it's your time, then it's your time." Who understands that lesson at 8 years old? I just wanted to be mad! LOL!

Lesson from Mommy

Who ALWAYS says
"There's a lesson in EVERYTHING!"

Be happy for other people's successes, AND AT THE RIGHT *time,* God will bring your dreams to pass.

Another acting OMG moment was when I didn't get a part in The Little Mermaid. I didn't know why. Was it my singing? Was it my acting? When I was singing, all the judges were smiling. Oh well, I'm going to keep finding auditions until I finally get one, because I know not to give up and always to work hard. At the end of the day, I gotta let it go and keep DREAMING! I'm still mad though! LOL! Mom says, I have a right to be mad but I have to look forward.

My acting coach, Mr. Brian said "It's all part of the acting process!! But I'm gonna continue to work with you to help you become more prepared". Thanks Mr. Brian!!!

Chapter 4

#TeriseTheGiver

I know it's important to give because people or kids that are in the hospital need to feel happy. My mom and I decided we would do a book drive and donate the books to a woman and children's shelter and Believe in Tomorrow (They work with the Children's Hospital of Johns Hopkins). I hope my books will make them stop thinking about being in a hospital and be  happy while reading them. We had so many books. We also gave some to Mr. Shelley of Shelley's Helping Hands. He does Books N BBQ, a FREE event where people can get food and books, every summer in Baltimore City.

I asked my church, my school and my dance studio to help me collect books. I was so happy when I heard back from the hospital that the kids loved the books. So I donated again in 2015. This time we had over 700 books!! Then they asked me if I wanted a TOUR of the hospital. I'm going to do what I like & keep giving.

My Taekwondo Teacher, Mr. Tony, reminded me that giving is more than just giving "stuff". People can give money, time or advice. So one Saturday afternoon, I went to the Kids Safe Zone, in Baltimore, where all the riots happened in April 2015. They made the Kids Safe Zone so the kids could play and be safe and sound. I was there to do story time, since I LOVE to read!! I read to them when I first came in and I even gave them some books I had from my book drive. It looked very pretty inside the Safe Zone. I saw a lot of posters on the wall, pictures the kids drew, a lot of

Xbox's, computers, Wii games AND board games. I didn't wanna leave. Hopefully, they will want to ask me to come back there again!

<u>Update from Mommy</u> Giving to others is a lesson I truly want Terise to understand. Our Pastor, Apostle Karen, says that when you GIVE or SERVE, there are 3 areas that should always benefit from, your gifts, family, church and your community. Therefore, a portion of all book sales will be donated to a local charity. #iGive #iServe #BlessedToBeABlessing

Chapter 5

#TeriseTheOvercomer

My Taekwondo teacher suggested to my mom that we put this chapter in the book. Alright guys, this is a HARD chapter for me but here we go...... Hi. my name is Terise and I HAD seizures! I kinda hate that word, but there ..... I said it!!

This part of the chapter I only know because my mom told me. I first had seizures when I was 3 years old and they all happened whenever I was awake, during the day. God healed me for 5 years, but then next thing you know, when I was 8 years old my mom woke up one morning and saw me having one in my SLEEP! She said I had a new seizure in my sleep like almost every 2 weeks. For 6 months, mommy said it was REALLY HARD for her to sleep at night, especially since it's just me and her at home. She's a single mom. I definitely couldn't go to any sleepovers at my friend's house and she had to buy a baby monitor for my room just to watch me at night. But **THANK GOD** that I am healed now. I haven't had any seizures in 6 months as of October 2015!

When I had seizures I hated the whole process because I had to ride in the ambulance to the hospital, get shots and the WORSE PART WAS THE MEDICINE! Because the seizures were at night, I had to take medicine twice in the evening. My doctor said I needed it before I went to sleep to protect me. The 1ST medicine was okay, but the 2ND one was HORIBBLE! IT LOOKED LIKE MILK and IT MADE ME WANNA PUKE. I also had to take a pill, but I was able to take it with applesauce or yogurt because I didn't know how to swallow a pill yet. When I had to take medicine in front of everyone, it's kinda embarrassing because I had to stop what I was doing to take it. I was embarrassed because everyone would crowd me sometimes and then they ALWAYS ask a bunch of questions like "What is that?", and "Why do you have to take it"?

The first medicine that my doctor gave me made me cry and sad A LOT. If I didn't get my way, I would cry and whine. My mom didn't like "sad Terise", she liked the happy one. I remember watching the Disney movie "Inside Out" (Google it) where Sadness was always sad... I felt the same way. I used to call my dad and start to cry and he would say "Why you acting like that, yo"?? (He says "yo" A LOT ... LOL).....but he didn't understand. We had to call Dr. Shafrir and switch the medicine to a different one. But the new one made me hungry, LOL. Mommy had to make sure we had healthy snacks in the house and lots of water.

Because the seizures were happening a lot, my mom had to tell EVERYONE that I was having them. OMG, so embarrassed again. I know it's for my own good so that they can be aware. We had to tell my school nurse, the people at Children's Church, my babysitter that I go to when school is closed, all my teachers at dance, Pastor, mommy even had a meeting with my teachers and principals at school.

I had to have **A LOT** of tests done. I went to my neurologists office to have an EEG done (don't know what that means) but my mom said the kid meaning is "sleep study". The nurse had to take my hair out and put this red crayon in my scalp so they could see where to put the sensors. They put some lotion and glue in my hair to hold the sensors. The nurse turned the lights out to make me fall asleep and she even put a picture on the ceiling that looked like Nemo the clown fish and Dori the blue fish. The picture was even glowing in the dark. I had to sleep for like 40 minutes. My mom stayed in the room with me and all the doctors watched me from another room. They wanted to see what my brain was doing while I was asleep.

This part my mom had to tell me, but she said the results weren't good. This part makes me sad all over again, but they put me on a "Watch and Wait" List. Mommy said that my brain showed a lot of seizure activity and the Doctor said she should just "watch" me and "wait" to see if I had more. I did ® and that's why Dr. Shafrir put me on medicine.

So it's the first day of spring break 2015 and the doctors have to take blood from me...... More tests!! I'M MAD!!! Not fun at all. I'm supposed to be having spring break fun, but no, it's the worst day ever, no fair! Then, mommy tells me I have a MRI on the 13th! "Seriously, WHY?" I know it will make me better, but I don't feel like doing any of this...but I still smile...sometimes.

Monday, the 13th of April 2015 is here, spring break is over and I'm gonna be late for school ..... why?? Cuz I have to have a MRI, a machine that takes pictures of my brain. I don't like taking the MRI because it's a lot of loud noises that make my ears POP! I also

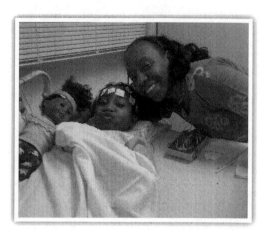

have to take my hair out of my puffs before I go in the machine.

I'm really nervous because I don't know how long it'll take. It's gonna be scary going in that machine. Right now, I feel like I wanna throw something. My mom reminded me that today is the 13th and in 4 days, April 17th, I celebrate 1 month of having no seizures!! So ok.... now I feel happy because I know that God is HEALING ME! AND my MRI and blood tests all came back NORMAL!

I know now that salads and green foods help my brain and I have to do my part and eat more salads and drink water. The medicine is also working... YAY!! The medicine is telling my brain and the seizures to STOP!! So, anybody and I mean ANYBODY who is going through anything, read this chapter, #TeriseTheOvercomer. It's powerful, and if you see a difference in your life, God is healing you too.

I like going to Dr. Shafrir's office, my neurologist. He's nice, but mommy said "Yes, he's nice, but I don't want to see him anymore, cause if we have to go and see him more that means you're not getting better." My Pastor and

Elder Jan prayed for me and gave me healing scriptures to look over and say every day. My mom even took a bible study class at our church called the "Healing Clinic". She really wanted me better. The seizures are really getting better. I haven't had any in over 6 months. Thanks to everyone that prayed over me and thank you God for healing me!!!

Lesson from Terise

My lesson for this chapter and for people that are going through stuff like seizures or cancer, is do EVERYTHING that you can to make you feel better and let God do the rest !! My FAVORITE song that I listened to that made me feel better was "Overcomer" by Mandisa .

Scripture reference from Mommy – Matthew 4:23-35

Chapter 6

~

Mommy's Chapter - #TheProudMom

Where do I even begin…

Early one October morning, I woke up to Terise having a convulsive seizure in her sleep. Besides losing my mom when I was 17, this was the worst experience in my life EVER!! I had never seen anything like that before, and prayed to never see it again. Unfortunately, like you read in Chapter 5, the seizures, in her sleep nonetheless, went on for 6 loooooong months. Seizures affect the brain and the neurology system. During this difficult time, I tried so hard to find the "Why"!! Why was this happening to her again? Why in her sleep? Why Lord, why? It is SO CLEAR to me now. The bible says in John 10:10, that "the enemy comes to steal, kill and destroy". The enemy knew that it was not only

Terise's plan, but also God's plan to write and publish this book. So in true enemy form, he tried to attack her brain so that this book, and all her dreams, would never manifest. During this time, the enemy also tried to stop me…. And I was almost willing to let him. I was super stressed out, tired from lack of sleep (watching Terise as she slept of course) and burnt out from all the Dr's visits she had to have. I was ready to give up, throw in the towel and keep Terise home from everything!!! No Dance, No Taekwondo…….. Nothing but school. Thank God, however, for my close knitted family and friends circle, my therapist Dr Gwen (she's the best) that encouraged me to push through this rough season. Thank God for my Pastor and Elder Jan, everyone at church and all of my family and friends who prayed with us and for us.

March 17th, 2015…… FINALLY, it all came to an end. That was the day of her last episode!!! Thank God Terise and I serve a mighty God that not only healed her, but also gave her all the words, and then some, for this project.

REJOICE IN OUR CONFIDENT HOPE.
BE PATIENT
IN TROUBLE,
and
KEEP ON PRAYING

ROMANS 12:12

When Terise first approached me with the idea to write a book, I was driving. I tried to focus on the road, but also wanted to make sure I heard her correctly. "A book"? On top of dancing, modeling, acting, Taekwondo, and all the many other things Terise does, I wasn't ready, but I knew that this wasn't the end of the conversation.

This Chapter is called "Proud Mom", but honestly, I am amazed, speechless, and often times brought to tears when I think of where God has brought Terise from and where he is taking her to. Every time I see her on stage at a recital, break a board at Taekwondo, remember her lines in a play, I get filled with the greatest joy a mother could ever experience for their child. As much as this book is for you, the readers, to be inspired, this book & Terise has also, in **so many ways,** has inspired me. My take away from this book is for everyone to go for ALL the dreams, visions, goals and thoughts that you may have! Be unstoppable in your efforts to "make it (whatever IT may be for you) happen" & let God direct you towards greatness.

Being a single mom and rearing a child that has a new thought and idea every other minute, LOL, is not easy! However, without overwhelming myself or Terise, I do whatever is in budget, activities that will bring out her God given talent, and also those where she can learn and have fun. At the end of the day, I have to remind myself that she is just 8 years old and having fun is allowed☺. Terise loves performing arts. It's in her DNA. I look forward to the day where I can sit back and support her during her Broadway debut or accepting her first Tony award or Oscar. The book is called #DreamBigNeverSmall ,right?

To all my parents reading this book, I can't stress enough how important it is to support your children and their endeavors. Expose them to new things, be it sports, acting, music, swimming, gymnastics, etc. We need to be our kids biggest cheerleader. I once heard the owner of Studio "A", Ms. Adrienne say (when it comes to our kids) "Make a BIG DEAL out of everything"!! And I so agree. We have to let them know that we love them, support them, and want to see them succeed. If, as parents, we do that, the future of not only our kids, but the world, looks bright, as we assist in raising mathematicians, engineers, book authors... HELLO.... dancers, or even the next President of the United States.

And remember parents, as much of a responsibility we have in helping our kids succeed and encourage them to go for their dreams, it is okay to do the same for ourselves. It's just as important for our kids to be proud of us as we are of them! Now, with that being said, I have some goals I need to accomplish!!

#MyDailyReminder #MyDaughterInspirsesMe
#DreamBigAndNeverSmall

Chapter 7

#InspirationReallyIsEverywhere

The person who inspired me as an actor was Quvenzhane' Wallis from the movie Annie. We're similar cause we're both black girls and we are close in age. I'm 8 and she's 12. She inspired me to be in movies like her. When I saw the movie I felt sad she didn't' have any parents, so that means I have to be grateful for mine. That movie was AMAZING, I loved it!!

The other movie that inspired me was The Gabby Douglas story. One day she kept breaking stuff around the house doing cartwheels. She wanted to be a gymnast but she had to train to get to the Olympics. It took a couple of months for her to get there, but she had to leave her family. Gabby was excited to move and get started with a famous coach. She missed her family a lot though. She even wanted to QUIT!! Her brother got really mad about that.

Her mom said "You can't quit, you wanted to do this for years". Gabby pushed herself and made it all the way to the Olympics.

Lesson from Terise

Even if you have to move away from your family .... GO FORWARD and get focused on your DREAM. Gabby had a supportive family. If you have a supportive family, that's really good because it's a good feeling and family can motivate you, even if you want to quit.

I heard my daddy playing this song one day called "I Know I Can" by Nas. I think he likes this song because Nas is from Queens, just like him, and he likes rap music. The song means you can be **ANYTHING** you wanna be, even an author at 8 years old like **ME.**☺ ☺ #TeriseTheAuthor . The song also says you can be a TV actress, a doctor or a ballerina.... I like that part !! #BrownGirlsDoBallet

My favorite part of the song is when he says **"Nothing comes easy, it takes much practice"**!! That's so true. You have to work hard to make your dreams come true. I want my readers to know that **INSPIRATION** really is everywhere, just like mommy reminds me all the time, even in a song and movie!!

I met Gabrielle Jordan at an event in DC. She was selling jewelry that she makes and her book that she wrote, and I was a model in the fashion show. I even got my nails done and danced at the event. We all had on PJ's too. Gabrielle is my inspiration because I said "If she can write a book, I can too", plus she's a mature example for me. She was even on #BlackGirlsRock with #MichelleObama.

I saw Gabrielle again at another event in Baltimore. I got her autograph, 2 magazines she was in and the book she wrote.

My mom told me that a lot of famous people were born in Queens, NY. Both of my parents are from Queens.

It's inspiring because people who were born in Queens are now doing BIG THINGS!! Now I can **#DreamBIG** and be successful just like them.

****List of famous people from Queens, New York, added by Mom****

(Sidenote – Terise knows some of these celebs, others we will use as a future mommy / daughter History Lesson)

- Nas – rapper
- Run DMC – Rap Group
- Russell Simmons – Mogul / Fashion Designer / Def Jam Record Label Founder
- Tika Sumpter – Actress / "The Haves and the Haves Nots" (Tyler Perry)
- Al Rocker – NBC Today Show weatherman
- Lamar Odom – LA Lakers
- LL Cool J – Rapper
- Lucy Liu – Actress / Kill Bill
- Louis Armstrong – Jazz Musician
- Nicki Minaj – Rapper

The next list consists of former residents that lived in the hometown of Terise's parents, East Elmhurst, Queens:

- Langston Hughes – Poet
- Jackie Robinson – Baseball Player in the Negro League
- Eric Holder – Former US Attorney General

Are you inspired yet?? Good …. It's homework time…………..

Inspiration Homework

Write down 5 things or people that <u>INSPIRE</u> you. Here's my List!!

1. New York City lights _____

2. Art that looks weird_____

3. People Making a difference_____

4. Seeing the world change –
   Baltimore Riots / Pres. Obama _____

5. My Mommy_____

Now .....Write Yours .... Ready, Set, GO !!

1. _____

2. _____

3. _____

4. _____

5. _____

Chapter 8

#TeriseTheArtistAndOrangeBelt

(My other Hobbies & Gifts from God)

I LOVE to draw because it's creative and fun. I have a whole art wall of all my projects. I just couldn't stop the marker from moving half of the time. I don't know what I'm drawing sometimes until I'm done.

I go to Michael's to get my supplies and to get all the stuff that I need to help me be creative. I have markers, color pencils, crayons, paint, and a sketch book. I go on Google and YouTube to look up things to draw. My mom found this place called Artsy Partsy. I go there for "Pizza and Paint" night. It's so fun!!

I take Taekwondo every day after school and in the summer. I never wanted to take class in the summer cuz I do it over the school year. Right now, I'm an Orange Belt. I broke 3 boards and got a yellow with white stripe belt, then yellow with orange stripe belt and now just orange. Mr. Tony worked with me over the summer to get me ready for my next belt, Orange with white stripe and then GREEN BELT!! A belt is a HUGE responsibility!! You can't leave it on the floor EVER! It's disrespectful to the belt. You can't wash it, even if it's dirty or bloody. It shows your hard work!

When I do my Taekwondo tests, I am scared I won't get my moves correct. I thought I wouldn't break the board but I DID!! Some of the bigger kids were crying because they didn't break the board and didn't get their new belt, so they had to test the following week.

I put Taekwondo on my vision board. I will earn a Black Belt. Its hard work and lots of dedication. You have to be serious about it if you want to make it. The Taekwondo Motto is "Honesty, Loyalty, Confidence, and Dedication". That's what we say when class is over. So whenever you are testing, about to break a board, or taking class, you have to have all that in mind. I have a long way to go from Orange to Black Belt but my mom didn't sign me up for nothing. She wants me to learn how to be tough for a bully or a criminal.

When parents need to come to Mr. Tony to talk to him about their child, he takes it very serious. He doesn't play or laugh. You never know, he can move you down a level if you have bad behavior because he doesn't tolerate that. Mr. Tony is strict, nice

#TeriseTheOrangeBelt

and supportive. He's strict because you have to take Taekwondo seriously. You never know who is ready to fight you. You can't laugh and you have to pay attention or you can get a black eye if you don't block properly. #ThatsNotCute. If you are doing your moves wrong or weak, it's a problem. Mr. Tony be like "Come on son".... (to all the boys) "Do it stronger than that or drop down and give me 10 pushups"!!

Mr. Tony cares about us and wants us to feel protected. He says if someone is defending you in real life and its two people, you have to choose which one to fight OR you should pack your things and RUN. #ThatsFunny #HeWasSerious

Chapter 9

Learning to Ride My Bike

The other issue I have to overcome is that my dad lives in New York and I live in Maryland. I'm sad about that! I have to travel to see him. I know he loves me but I wanna be around him more. Being a child of divorced parents is hard for an 8 year old; not to see their daddy is tough. I wanna love mommy and daddy together. I may be a divorced child but that doesn't mean I don't have my dad.

I love it when he calls me every day and comes over to play with me. He taught me how to play chess, act silly (we drive mommy crazy....LOL), and do art together. One time when he came to Maryland, he even took me to the Daddy / Daughter event.

Lesson from Terise

Even if you are a divorced child, your parents still loves you, even if you are far away.

My dad came to Maryland to buy me a bike w/o training wheels. I was so excited to have a BIG GIRL bike, but scared because I wasn't sure if I could do it. I tried and tried, but I still couldn't do it. I wanted to ride my bike so bad the next day. This time I GOT IT!! I was so fast I could feel the wind blowing when the sun was out. I stopped a couple of  times but if my bike slowed down I kept pushing. When I kept doing that I did four good laps. Mom said it's time to go inside. I said "I love my new bike". I learned to ride my bike in two days. At first, I couldn't hear mommy when she said stop and I didn't know how to brake. It was kinda hot outside, so I drank a lot of water. I kept trying and trying until I got it. Once I finally did it without stopping, I was so HAPPY I did cartwheels, a toe touch, the Whip and the Nae Nae, LOL! I was having a good 'ole time!! I was really sad when I didn't get it at first, but I said, "I can do it". I kept saying that to myself, to the point where I became a PRO!!

What I learned riding my bike is to overcome your fears and learn new things. You can accomplish anything. I was scared at first, but I'm not anymore. I was afraid of letting go. I thought I was going to fall, but I didn't.

Lesson from Terise

The key detail is it doesn't matter if you keep falling or wobbling because I did that when I first got the bike. But I had to control the bike. I turned, it turned....

So when I got it, I just said "Dream BIG Terise", "you can do this". I wanted to keep that in my head. Just

like when my mom was helping me,
sometimes all you need is one
big PUSH, and then gooooo!
Now I can ride, on my own!!

Chapter 10

~

#MyFinalMessage

Now that you read my book, you know my dreams and my goals and all the things I want to accomplish.

I'm always …

Dreaming BIG
and never SMALL.

I also put God and the Holy Spirit in my life to make all the life challenges that are hard… easy. I pray every night before bed, and I keep trying to accomplish my goals every day. Dancing, Modeling & Acting is helping me to be a Broadway Star. In order to do that, I have to say I can do whatever I put my mind to.

I pray that if you are reading this book and struggling with something, to keep trying, never GIVE UP, dream BIG and say, "I CAN DO IT", and hopefully you will accomplish all of your goals. I hope you all enjoyed this book and got the message and the whole purpose of the book. THANK YOU again, to Gabrielle Jordan, my inspiration. She's 15 years old now and wrote her book when she was 11. You should Google her or follow her on Instagram @GabrielleJordanInspires. I want you all to keep in touch with me too. All my social media (Facebook, Twitter, Instagram and Youtube) are under @ThisisTerise. My website is www.thisisterise.com and you can email me at thisisterise@aol.com. I hope you guys write back saying that you liked the book. I hope I encouraged someone to Dream BIG and Never Small. Amen!!

34238576R00035